To Rachel — J.C.

For Belinda, Bethany and Arby — B.W.

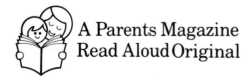 A Parents Magazine
Read Aloud Original

Golly Gump Swallowed a Fly

by Joanna Cole
pictures by Bari Weissman

Parents Magazine Press • New York

Publication licensed by Gruner + Jahr USA Publishing

Text Copyright © 1981 by Joanna Cole.
Illustrations Copyright © 1981 by Bari Weissman.
All rights reserved. Printed in the United States of America.
10   9   8   7

Library of Congress Cataloging in Publication Data
Cole, Joanna. Golly Gump swallowed a fly.
SUMMARY: A prize-winning yawner encounters
steadily increasing troubles as he tries to get
rid of the fly he accidentally swallows.
I.   Weissman, Bari, ill.   II.   Title.
PZ7.C67346Go   [E]   81-11072
ISBN 0-8193-1069-7   AACR2
ISBN 0-8193-1070-0   (lib. bdg.)

Golly Gump Swallowed a Fly

When Golly Gump went to the fair,
he won first prize for yawning.

Golly Gump was the best yawner for miles around.
His yawn was wider, and taller, and louder
than anyone else's.

When he got home, Golly put his prize
on the gatepost and started swinging
back and forth, yawning, and yawning.

As he was swinging, a fly flew by.
Just at that moment, Golly yawned
his first-prize yawn. And...

I don't know how, I don't know why,
But Golly Gump swallowed that fly!

Now Golly was in trouble.
He could feel that fly inside him
buzzing round and round.

He didn't know what to do.
He jumped off the garden gate

and ran up the road yelling.
But that didn't help.

So he asked himself a question:
"What catches flies?"
And he told himself the answer:
"Spiders!"

Then Golly knew just what to do.

He opened wide, he opened wider,
And Golly Gump swallowed a spider.

Then Golly was in a pickle again.
He could feel the spider tickling him inside.
But the fly must have been
too fast for the spider,
because he could still feel the fly too,
buzzing round and round.

Now Golly didn't like that one bit.
He leaped up and ran down the road again.
But when that didn't help,
he sat down and began to think.

He asked himself a question.
"What catches spiders?"
And he told himself the answer:
"Birds."

So Golly did what he had to do.

It's the silliest thing I ever heard,
But Golly Gump swallowed a bird!

Poor Golly! That made things worse than ever.
He could feel the bird flapping inside.
But he could still feel the spider tickling him,
and the fly was buzzing round and round.

That made Golly really mad.
He was so mad he didn't even have
to ask himself a question.
He knew what catches birds, all right.
Cats!

So he knew what to do right away.

Don't ask me how he managed that,
But Golly Gump swallowed a cat!

Oh boy! Golly was in bad trouble now.
He could hear that cat meowing inside,
and feel the bird flapping,
and the spider tickling him with its long legs,
and the fly buzzing round and round.
That's a lot going on in one person's stomach!

Just then, a yellow dog came down the road, stopping at every tree to sniff.

Can you guess what Golly did next?

Old Golly acted like a hog,
And swallowed down that yellow dog.

Then you should have heard the noise!
The dog was howling,
the cat was yowling,
the bird was flapping,
the spider was tickling,
and the fly was buzzing round and round.

Now Golly swallowed the very next thing
he saw coming down the road.

Do you know what it was?

It was someone big, it was someone tall,
It was the dog catcher, net and all!

Now Golly was in the worst trouble yet.
Inside was the dog catcher yelling,
  the dog howling,
    the cat yowling,
      the bird flapping,
        the spider tickling,
and the fly still buzzing round and round.

It felt like a zoo in there.

Golly thought until his brain was all worn out.
But he couldn't think of anything that
catches dog catchers.

He was afraid he would have to walk around
for the rest of his life with a zoo inside.
Then he asked himself a question:
"What is really scary?"
And then he stood up and he yelled
his loudest yell.

Well, that scared 'em!

Golly opened wide
and they all ran out—
the dog catcher yelling,

the dog howling,
  the cat yowling,
    the bird flapping,
      the spider tickling,
and the fly buzzing round and round.

They all disappeared down the road
in a cloud of dust,
and Golly started home.

He felt so much better without all that company
in his stomach.

Golly Gump did learn one thing from all that fuss.
He learned to cover his mouth when he yawned.
And that's something to know.

ABOUT THE AUTHOR

JOANNA COLE likes visiting county fairs.
Although she has never seen a yawning
contest, she saw an interesting ox-pulling
contest once. "The farmers hitched teams of
two oxen to great weights, then the oxen
that pulled farthest won," she says. "Some
farmers whipped their animals a little
to start off. But the one who won just
whispered in his oxen's ears!"

Ms. Cole was an elementary school
teacher and a children's book editor before
turning to writing children's books full
time. *Golly Gump Swallowed A Fly* is her
second book for Parents, following *The
Clown-Arounds*.

Ms. Cole lives with her husband and
daughter and their Yorkshire Terrier in
New York City. She says they all have good
manners and cover their mouths when they
yawn—except for the Yorkshire Terrier,
that is.

ABOUT THE ARTIST

BARI WEISSMAN did the sketches for *Golly Gump* on her back porch. "There was always a fly there, buzzing around me," she says. "I started to feel like Golly. It's a good thing I never yawned!"

Ms. Weissman has illustrated several picture books, one of which she also wrote. Two of them are about flies. "I guess I just draw them to me," she says. *Golly Gump Swallowed A Fly* is the first book she has illustrated for Parents.

Ms. Weissman lives with her husband and their black and white cat, Oboe, in Brighton, Massachusetts.